ELIE SIEGMEIST

AMERICAN KALEIDOSCOPE

CONTENTS

Editor: James L. King III
Production Coordinator: Karl Bork
Art Design: Michael Ramsay

© 1955, 1962 Sam Fox Publishing Company, Inc.
Copyrights Renewed and Assigned to WB MUSIC CORP.
All Rights Reserved including Public Performance

MARCH

ELIE SIEGMEISTER

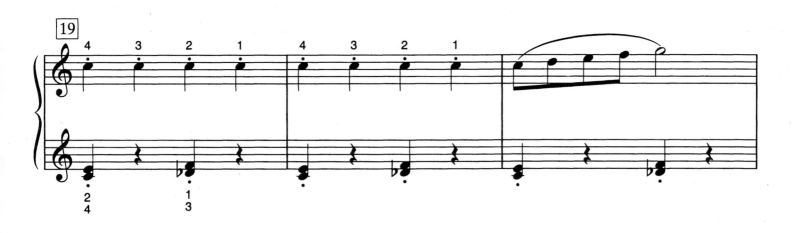

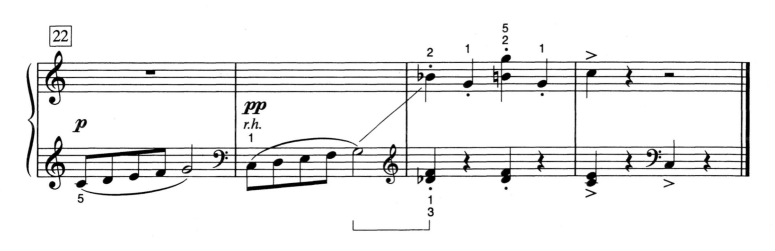

BANJO TUNE

ELIE SIEGMEISTER

Lively, with a strong beat

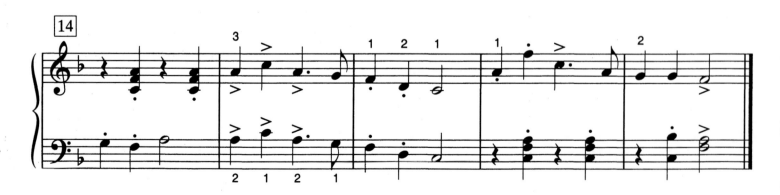

SONG OF THE DARK WOODS

ELIE SIEGMEISTER

ELM03017

A BIT OF JAZZ

ELIE SIEGMEISTER

STREET GAMES

ELIE SIEGMEISTER

Rough and tough

BOOGIE

ELIE SIEGMEISTER

BLUES

ELIE SIEGMEISTER

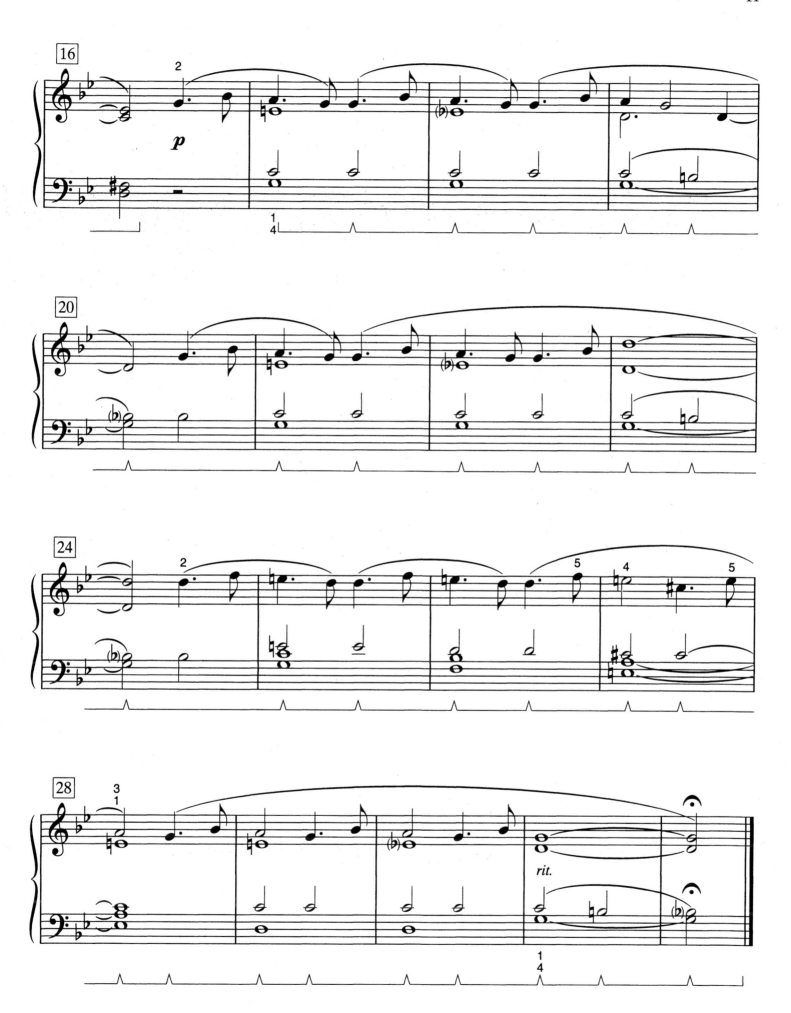

PRAIRIE NIGHT

ELIE SIEGMEISTER

OLD TIME DANCE

ELIE SIEGMEISTER

FAIRY TALE

ELIE SIEGMEISTER

THE TOY RAILROAD

ELIE SIEGMEISTER

FEELING EASY

ELIE SIEGMEISTER

BOOGIE RHYTHM

ELIE SIEGMEISTER

FOLLOW THE LEADER

ELIE SIEGMEISTER

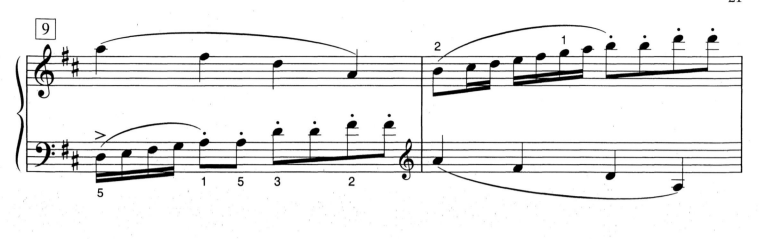

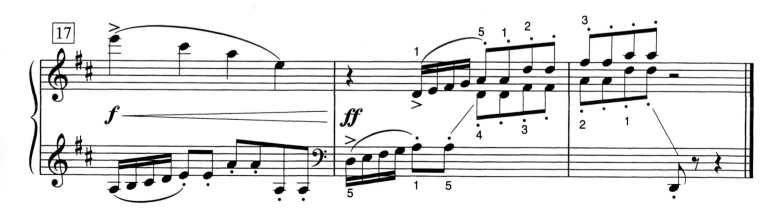

BICYCLE WHEELS

ELIE SIEGMEISTER

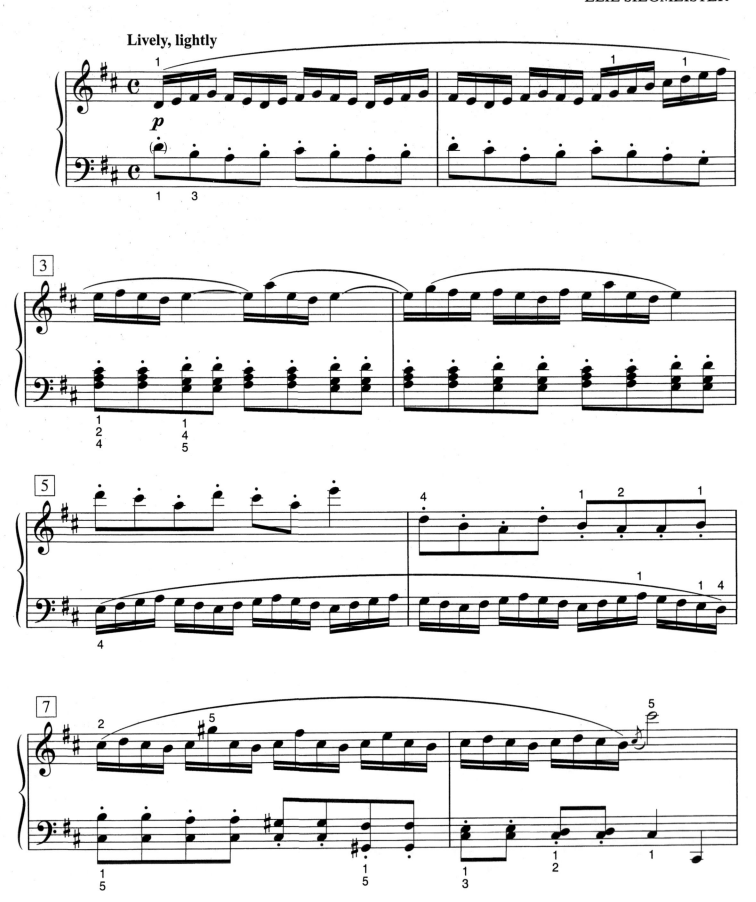

MARCHING

ELIE SIEGMEISTER

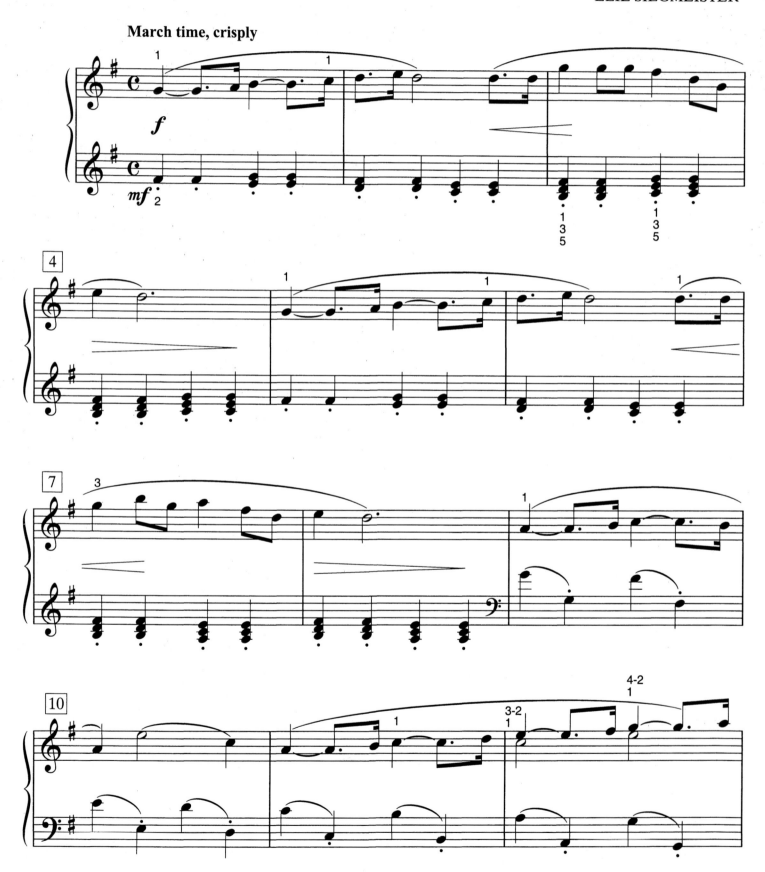

MONKEY BUSINESS

ELIE SIEGMEISTER

SUNNY DAY

ELIE SIEGMEISTER

*First use the thumb to play both the G and A, then substitute fingers 2 and 3.

THE CHASE

ELIE SIEGMEISTER

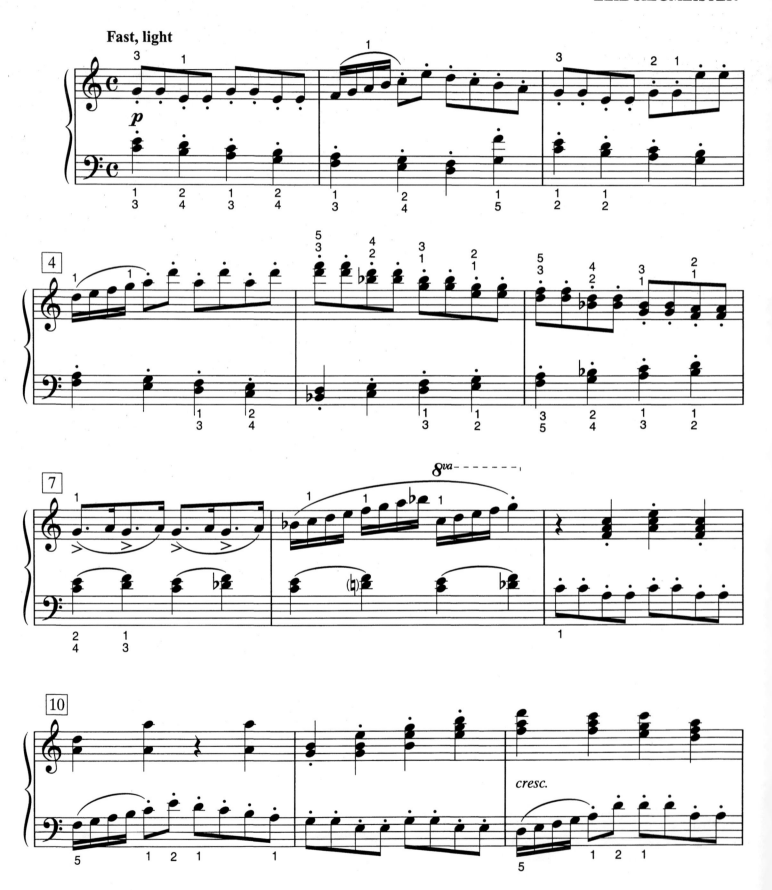

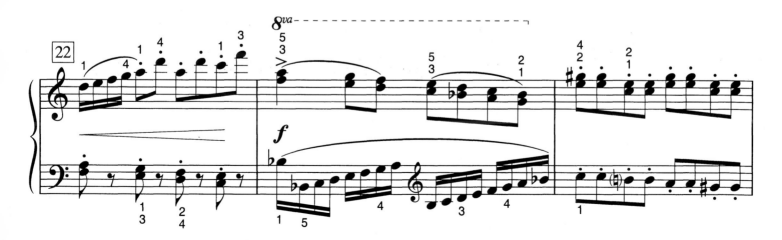